Knit Now

BY MEGAN E. BRYANT

ILLUSTRATED BY LINDA KARL
PHOTOGRAPHY BY DAVID MAGER/PEARSON LEARNING GROUP

PRICE STERN SLOAN

FOR VICTORIA, WHO TAUGHT ME
HOW TO KNIT WHEN I NEVER
THOUGHT I COULD LEARN.
THANKS EVERMORE!—M.E.B.

SPECIAL THANKS TO SUPER-KNITTERS BONNIE BADER AND SHANE BREAUX.
COVER AND INTERIOR DESIGN: SHANE BREAUX AND ROSANNE GUARARRA

PRICE STERN SLOAN
Published by the Penguin Group
Penguin Group (USA) Inc., 375 Hudson Street, New York, New York 10014, U.S.A.
Penguin Group (Canada), 10 Alcorn Avenue, Toronto, Ontario, Canada M4V 3B2
(a division of Pearson Penguin Canada Inc.)
Penguin Books Ltd, 80 Strand, London WC2R 0RL, England
Penguin Ireland, 25 St Stephen's Green, Dublin 2, Ireland
(a division of Penguin Books Ltd)
Penguin Group (Australia), 250 Camberwell Road, Camberwell, Victoria 3124, Australia
(a division of Pearson Australia Group Pty Ltd)
Penguin Books India Pvt Ltd, 11 Community Centre, Panchsheel Park, New Delhi - 110 017, India
Penguin Group (NZ), Cnr Airborne and Rosedale Roads, Albany, Auckland 1310, New Zealand
(a division of Pearson New Zealand Ltd)
Penguin Books (South Africa) (Pty) Ltd, 24 Sturdee Avenue, Rosebank, Johannesburg 2196, South Africa

Penguin Books Ltd, Registered Offices:
80 Strand, London WC2R 0RL, England

Produced by Tony Potter Publishing Ltd., RH17 5PA, UK

ISBN 0-8431-1653-6
10 9 8 7 6 5 4 3 2

TABLE OF CONTENTS

Get KNitty!

WHY KNIT? WHY NOT! IT'S THE COOLEST HOBBY AND IT'S EASY TO LEARN. WHY PAY OUT YOUR HARD-EARNED CASH FOR THAT SLINKY SCARF OR STYLISH HAT? JUST LEARN TO KNIT AND YOU CAN MAKE THEM FOR YOURSELF—IN EXACTLY THE SIZE AND COLOR *YOU* WANT. KNITTED STUFF MAKES GREAT GIFTS FOR FAMILY AND FRIENDS, TOO. BETTER YET, GET YOUR BFFS TOGETHER AND START A KNITTING CLUB. YOU CAN SHARE TIPS, TRICKS, AND TALK AS YOUR NEEDLES ZOOM AND THE STITCHES FLY.

How to Use This Book

This book comes with two color-coded size 8 knitting needles, a yarn needle, and 50 yards of yarn. When you learn different knitting techniques, hold the green needle in your left hand and the pink needle in your right hand. That will make it easier to follow the diagrams. (The instructions and diagrams will still work if you aren't using the color-coded knitting needles, of course!)

There's enough yarn in this book to make the mini-purse, the cell phone pouch, the iPod case, the pom-pom, or the flower. For larger projects like the scarf, hat, and purse, you'll need to buy more yarn. Any yarn that works with size 8 needles will work for the patterns in this book! The yarn that comes with this book is 100 percent acrylic. It can be machine washed on the gentle cycle in warm or cold water—but don't use chlorine bleach! Also, don't iron this yarn.

Winding Yarn into a Ball

Before you start knitting, always wind the yarn into a ball, especially if it comes wrapped in a skein. This helps you see if any of the yarn is defective (dyed wrong or knotted up) before you start knitting. You can cut that section out now and you won't have any surprises later on. Most importantly, winding your yarn into a ball will keep it from getting all tangled up as you knit.

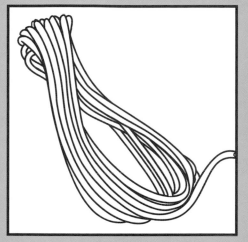

1. Untwist the skein until it is one big loop of yarn.

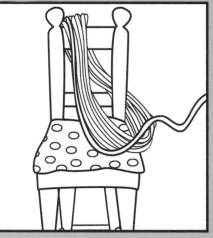

2. Then hang the skein over the back of a chair and start winding.

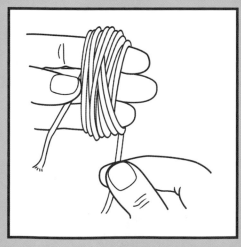

3. To wind yarn into a ball, start by wrapping it about 20 times around two or three of your fingers.

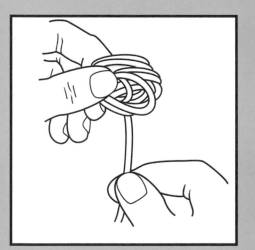

4. Slip this bunch of yarn off your fingers, and continue wrapping the yarn around in a different direction. When it gets thick, turn the ball and start wrapping the yarn in another direction. Keep turning the ball as you wind up the yarn. Now you're ready to knit!

COMMIT to KNIT!

THERE ARE LOTS OF DIFFERENT SUPPLIES KNITTERS CAN USE TO MAKE KNITTING EASY AND FUN! THE MOST IMPORTANT ONES (YARN AND NEEDLES) COME WITH THIS BOOK, AND AS YOU KNIT MORE, YOU CAN DECIDE IF YOU WANT TO EXPAND YOUR COLLECTION OF KNITTING SUPPLIES.

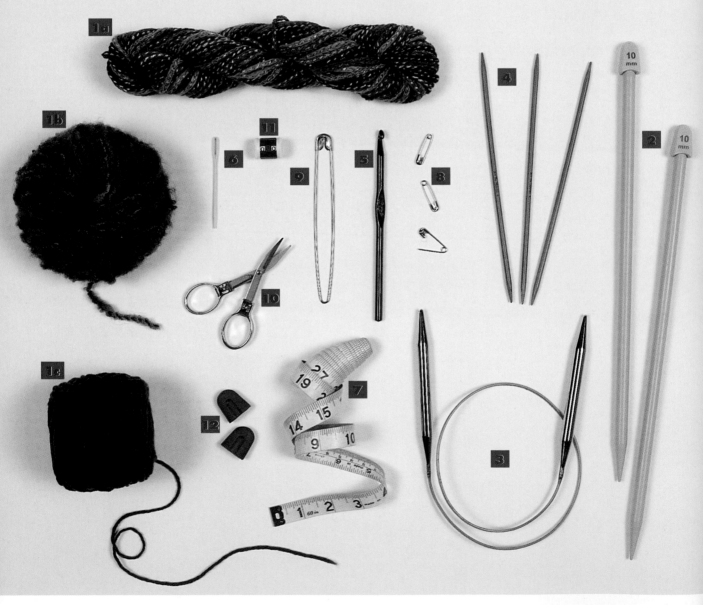

1. **Yarn** comes in all different colors, materials, and weights (*weight* means how thick the yarn is). The label on the yarn will tell you what it's made of, how to take care of it, and what size needles to use. **1a.** This is a skein of yarn—it will need to be wound into a ball before you can knit with it. Some knitting stores have skein winders that will do the work for you! (See photo 1c.) **1b.** This yarn has been wound into a big, round ball. **1c.** This yarn was wound in a knitting store using a skein winder. It looks different from a ball you'd wind yourself, but it will work just as well (and save you the trouble, too!).

2. **Straight needles** are exactly what they sound like—two straight, pointed knitting needles. They come in different lengths (from short to super-long) and sizes, from 000 (teeny tiny!) to 30 (huge!). The size needle you choose depends on the kind of yarn you use.

3. **Circular needles** are two shorter knitting needles connected by a thin plastic cord. When using circular needles, just flip the whole project around at the end of each row so the needle that was in your right hand is now in your left.

4. **Double-pointed needles** come in sets of four or five. Both ends of these needles are pointed, so that you can knit off of either end. You can use double-pointed needles to make hats or socks.

5. **Crochet hooks** are used for an entirely different craft—crocheting—but they can come in handy for knitters, too. You can use them to easily pick up dropped stitches, add fringe, or make a pretty chain of stitches to decorate your knitting.

6. **Yarn needles** come in plastic or steel—they are larger than sewing needles with a wider eye for the yarn. Use yarn needles to sew in the long tails of yarn at the ends of your projects and to sew seams.

7. **Tape measure**—this is a knitter's best friend! You can easily measure your yarn and your projects to ensure you're making the right size.

8. **Safety pins** are used to piece together the project before you sew it up. They'll help you sew nice, straight seams.

9. **Stitch holders** look like giant safety pins. If you need to knit just one part of your knitting (without casting off, or "ending," the rest of it), put the rest of the stitches on the stitch holder. If you only need to put a few stitches on a stitch holder, a large safety pin will work just fine.

10. **Scissors** are necessary to cut the yarn. Make sure they're sharp so that they make a nice, even cut through the yarn.

11. **Row counter**—this little plastic device is used to count how many rows you've done. It's really helpful when you're making stripes or a complicated pattern.

12. **Point protectors** can be popped onto the tips of your needles when you take your knitting on the go—they will keep your project from falling off the needle. They'll also keep you from poking someone with your needles!

Cast ON!

BEFORE YOU CAN KNIT, YOU'VE GOT TO HAVE STITCHES ON YOUR NEEDLE. CASTING ON PUTS THAT FIRST ROW OF STITCHES ON THE NEEDLE—AND THEN YOU CAN KNIT TO YOUR HEART'S CONTENT! HERE ARE INSTRUCTIONS FOR TWO EASY WAYS TO CAST ON. TRY THEM BOTH AND SEE WHICH ONE YOU LIKE BEST.

One-Needle Cast On

This is a really easy way to cast on your first row of stitches. After you've done it a few times, you'll never forget!

1. Make an L with your left hand. Hook the yarn around your index finger and thumb, with the tail end around the thumb and the long end (that's attached to the ball) around your index finger. (Make sure there's at least 18 inches of yarn hanging off your thumb.) Hold both ends of yarn under your other three fingers to keep it out of the way (you don't need to pull the yarn too tightly).

2. Hold a knitting needle in your right hand. Pull the yarn that's between your thumb and finger **down**—like you're pulling back a slingshot.

3. Now loop the needle **around** and **under** the yarn in front of your thumb.

4. Then loop the needle **around** and **under** the yarn in front of your index finger.

5. Last, bring the needle **down through** the yarn loop around your thumb. Move your thumb out of the way and pull both ends of the yarn until the loops around the needle are snug. You'll have two stitches on your knitting needle!

6. Repeat steps 1–5 until you have enough stitches cast on the needle. (The first time, you'll get two stitches on your needle. After that, you'll get one stitch. It's weird—but it works.)

KNIT IT!

Make sure you don't cast on your stitches too tightly—this will make it hard to knit your first row. The cast-on row should slide up and down the needle easily. If you find that you tend to cast on tightly, try holding two needles together when you cast on. Then you can slip one of the needles out and knit like normal.

8

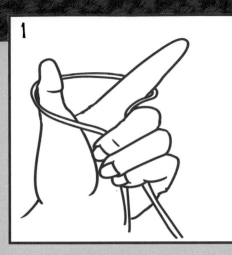

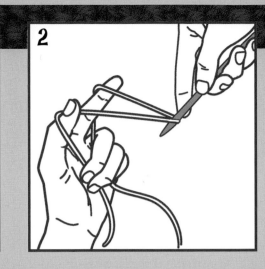

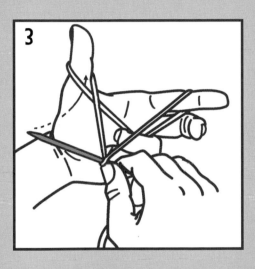

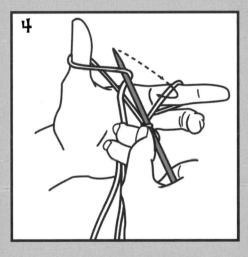

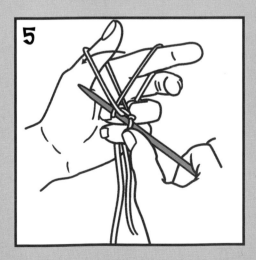

yippee!

Two-Needle Cast On

With this method, you actually knit to cast on—so it's a little easier to do once you've learned how to knit.

1. Make a slipknot.

1a. Loop the yarn around two fingers.

1b. Pinch the long tail of yarn and slip it through the loop around your fingers.

1c. Slip your fingers out of the loop. Hold the pinched yarn with one hand and pull the short tail with the other. Voilà—a loop with a flexible slipknot that lets you make the loop as big or as small as you want!

2. Put the slipknot on the needle and **pull the ends** in opposite directions so that the slipknot tightens around the needle.

3. Hold the needle with the slipknot in your left hand. Now start to knit the stitch: Put your right needle into the loop **under** the left needle so they cross to make an X.

4. Then loop the long tail **over** the right needle.

5. Bring the right needle **back through** the loop.

6. Hold it! Before you finish that knit stitch, pull the right needle toward you a little so the loop gets a bit larger. Then slip the loop from the right needle onto the left needle. Now you have two stitches!

7. Repeat steps 3–6 until you have as many stitches cast on as you want.

KNit Tip

With the one-needle cast on, the short tail of yarn will be in the same place as the long tail of yarn. With the two-needle cast on, the short tail of yarn will be at the opposite end of the needle.

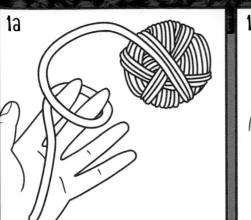

1a

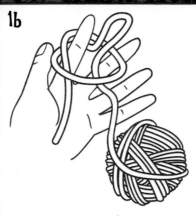

1b

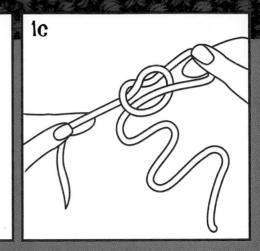

1c

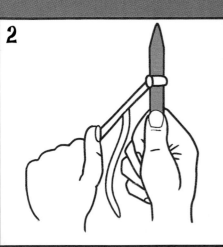

2

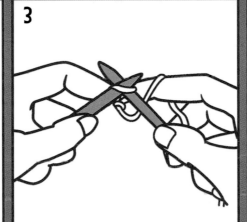

3

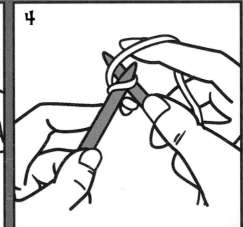

4

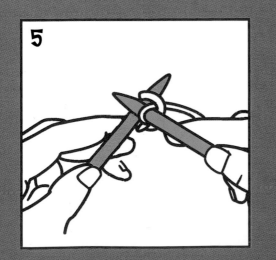

5

6

KNIT NOW

THIS IS IT—THE BIG KNIT STITCH! IT'S EASIER THAN YOU THINK, SO IF YOU DON'T GET IT AT FIRST, TRY AGAIN. YOU'LL SEE HOW QUICK IT IS TO PICK UP. WHEN YOU FIRST LEARN TO KNIT, IT'S A GOOD IDEA TO MAKE A PRACTICE PIECE. THIS GIVES YOU A CHANCE TO REALLY LEARN THE STITCHES, AND YOU CAN MAKE MISTAKES AS YOU LEARN WITHOUT WORRYING ABOUT HOW YOUR PROJECT WILL LOOK. WHEN YOU'RE DONE, YOU CAN SAVE THE PRACTICE PIECE OR RIP IT OUT AND REUSE THE YARN.

● ●

1. Cast on as many stitches as you need for your project. (If you're making a practice piece, 20 is a good number.)

2. There will be two tails of yarn hanging from the needle—a short one, and a long one connected to the ball of yarn. Ignore the short tail—you'll always use the long one to knit. The long tail of yarn will hang away from you, behind your needle.

3. Hold the needle with the cast-on stitches in your left hand.

4. Put the right needle into the first loop on the left needle. Both needles will be inside the same loop, and the right needle will cross **under** the left needle so that they make an X.

5. Loop the long tail of yarn **around** the right needle in a counterclockwise direction.

6. This part is a little tricky. Pull the right needle **back through** the loop—the same way it went in—while keeping the new loop of yarn around it. Your needle will make an X again—with the right needle on top.

7. Now use the right needle to slip the loop off the left needle and let it drop. That's it! You knit a stitch!

8. Repeat steps 4-7 until you get to the end of the row. Each time you knit a stitch off the left needle, it will show up on the right needle. When you knit the last stitch on the left needle, you'll find that they are all on the right needle. That means you knit a whole row. Yay, you!

9. Now what? Easy—just switch needles so that your right needle is now in your left hand and your left needle is in your right hand. All the stitches will be back in your left hand and you can knit away!

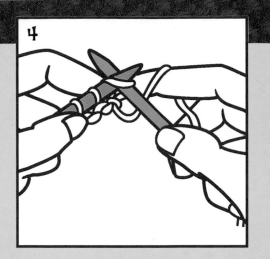

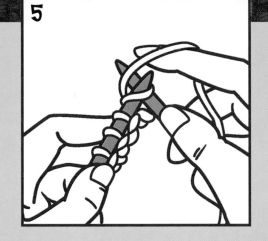

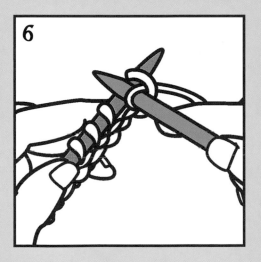

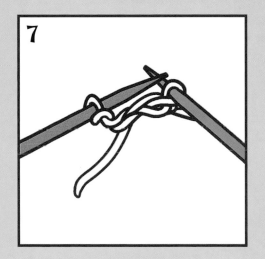

KNit Tip

How should you hold the long tail of yarn in your right hand? However feels comfortable to you! Some people like to wrap the yarn loosely around their fingers; that way, they can constantly feed it into their knitting. However, don't wrap the yarn too tightly around your fingers—you don't want to cut off circulation or make it feel uncomfortable or even have to keep stopping because your yarn is all tangled up in your fingers!

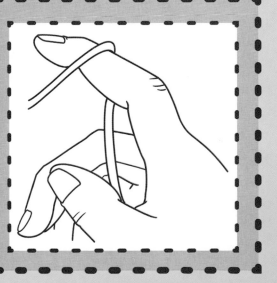

PURL Like a Pro

ALL OF THE AWESOME KNITTING PATTERNS IN THE WORLD USE ONLY TWO STITCHES—KNIT AND PURL. ONCE YOU CAN FLY THROUGH THE KNIT STITCH AND YOU UNDERSTAND IT INSIDE AND OUT, YOU'LL WANT TO LEARN HOW TO PURL. IT'S EASY AND IT OPENS UP A WHOLE WORLD OF KNITTING FUN! CHECK OUT SOME OF THE DIFFERENT COMBINATIONS FROM MIXING KNIT AND PURL STITCHES ON PAGE 24.

● ●

1. Cast on as many stitches as you need for your project. (If you're making a practice piece, 20 is a good number.)

2. There will be two tails of yarn hanging from the needle—a short one, and a long one connected to the ball of yarn. Ignore the short tail—you'll always use the long one.

3. Hold the needle with the cast-on stitches in your left hand. Hold the empty needle in your right hand.

4. Move the long tail of yarn **forward** so that it is in front of your stitches.

5. Now do the opposite of the knit stitch: Put the right needle through the first loop on the left needle, so that the right needle is **in front** of the left needle.

6. Loop the yarn **around** the right needle (that's why you need to have the yarn forward!) in a counterclockwise direction.

7. Bring the right needle **back through** the loop, out the same way it went in. Make sure you keep the new loop on the right needle!

8. Slip the first stitch off the left needle. That's it—you purled a stitch!

9. Repeat steps 5–8 for every stitch you want to purl.

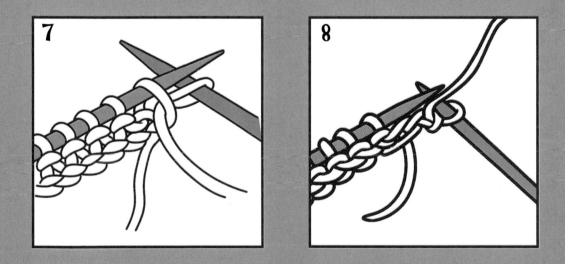

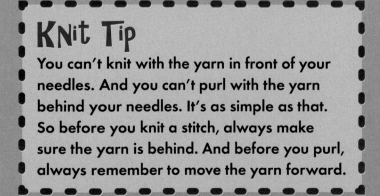

KNit Tip

You can't knit with the yarn in front of your needles. And you can't purl with the yarn behind your needles. It's as simple as that. So before you knit a stitch, always make sure the yarn is behind. And before you purl, always remember to move the yarn forward.

Cast Off

BEAUTIFUL! YOU'RE DONE WITH YOUR KNITTING PROJECT—EXCEPT FOR ONE PART. YOU DON'T WANT TO GO AROUND WITH A NEEDLE HANGING IN IT, RIGHT? AND YOU CAN'T JUST PULL THE NEEDLE OUT—THAT WOULD BE A KNITTING DISASTER. SO YOU'VE GOT TO CAST OFF—WHICH MEANS GETTING ALL THOSE STITCHES OFF THE NEEDLE AND SECURE ENOUGH TO STAND ON THEIR OWN.

1. Knit the first two stitches.

2. Put the left needle **into the loop** of the first stitch you knit (the one farthest away from the tip of the needle).

3. Use the left needle to bring the stitch **over** the one closest to the tip of the needle. It's like leapfrog for stitches.

4. Let the first stitch drop off the needle. Now you have only one stitch on your right needle.

5. Knit another stitch—there will be two stitches on your right needle again. Repeat steps 3 and 4.

6. Continue until there is only one stitch left on your right needle. Be careful—the knitted piece will get heavier as you cast off more of it, because all those stitches aren't supported by needles anymore.

7. Now switch hands so that you're holding the right needle in your left hand. Knit the one stitch left so that it's on the right needle again.

8. Pull the right needle **up** so that the stitch grows bigger and bigger.

9. Cut the yarn so that the tail is about 6 inches long, and keep pulling until the tail goes through the stitch. The stitch will turn into a tight little knot—and you're done casting off!

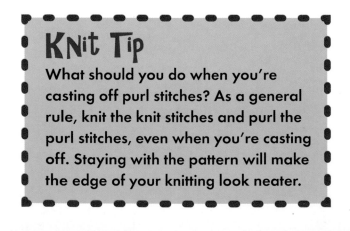

Knit Tip

What should you do when you're casting off purl stitches? As a general rule, knit the knit stitches and purl the purl stitches, even when you're casting off. Staying with the pattern will make the edge of your knitting look neater.

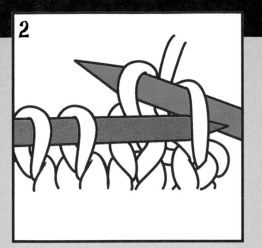

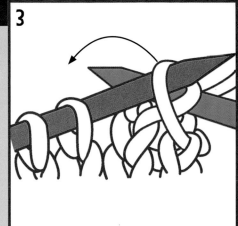

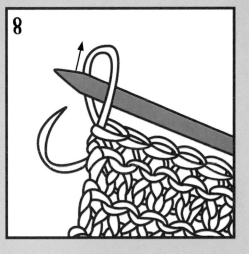

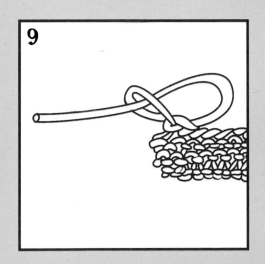

Sew What?

KNITTING REQUIRES SOME SIMPLE SEWING SKILLS—REALLY SIMPLE! FOR EVERY PROJECT YOU MAKE, NO MATTER HOW BASIC, YOU'LL WANT TO SEW IN THE TAILS OF YARN AT THE BEGINNING (WHERE YOU CAST ON) AND AT THE END (WHERE YOU CAST OFF) OF YOUR PROJECT.

Sewing in Ends

1. Thread the tail of yarn into a yarn needle.

2. Slip the needle under the closest stitch to the edge.

3. Weave the yarn in and out of the stitches for about 2 inches.

4. Carefully cut the yarn tail—it will disappear into the stitches.

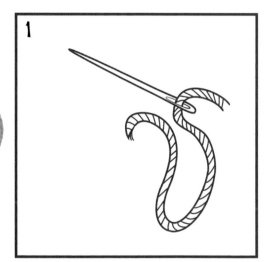

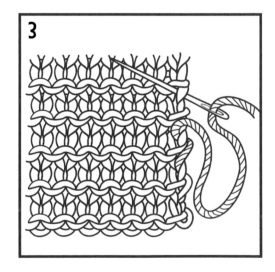

Sewing Seams

1. Line up both pieces of knitting and lay them out flat. If you're sewing a long seam, it's helpful to safety pin the pieces together.

2. Thread a yarn needle with yarn.

3. Put the yarn needle into the middle of the stitch at the bottom edge. Then put it through the middle of the stitch at the other bottom edge.

4. Gently pull the yarn, leaving a 3-inch tail at the end.

5. Now sew in the opposite direction: Put the needle through the middle of the edge stitch on the next row, then through the same stitch on the other side.

6. Continue like this until the two pieces are sewn together.

7. Sew in the yarn at either end of the seam. And you're done!

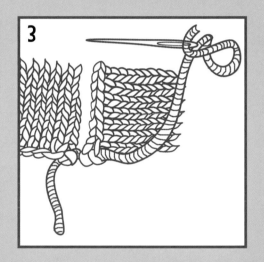

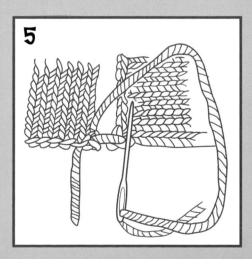

19

KNit iN the KNoW

If you have some problems with your knitting, don't throw a knit fit. It happens to everyone, and there's usually an easy fix to almost any problem! Read on for some tips and tricks—and if you still need help, don't hesitate to pop into a local knitting store. Most people who work in knitting stores are super-knitters who will be more than happy to get your knitting back on track.

● ●

Dropped Stitches

What it is: Oops! You started out with 10 stitches—and now you only have 9. And there's a funny hole that looks like the rungs of a ladder snaking down through your knitting!

What happened: At some point, one of the stitches fell off your needle. You'll need to weave it back through the other loops to make sure there are no holes in your knitting.

How to fix it: A crochet hook is like a magic wand for fixing this problem. Slip the crochet hook into the last normal stitch. Then put the crochet hook through the "rung" above it and slip the stitch over the rung. Keep doing this until you're at the top of your knitting; then slip the loop back onto the left needle. Then you can knit away—it's all fixed!

Dropped Stitch

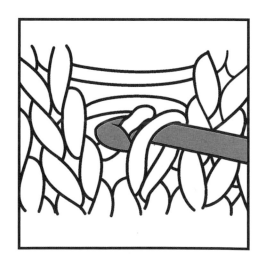

Extra Stitches

What it is: Uh-oh! You started out with 10 stitches—and now you have 11. And your knitting is suddenly wider than it used to be!

What happened: You probably added a stitch at one end of a row. This can happen whenever the yarn is looped over the needle in the front instead of hanging down in the back—it seems like the yarn is a real stitch, and it can accidentally be knit and become one.

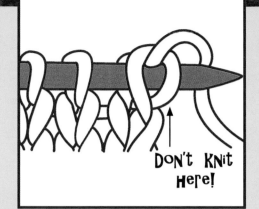

How to fix it: There's no quick fix for this one—you'll have to take out all the rows back to the one where your knitting suddenly gets wider. Read on to find out how!

Undoing a Few Stitches

What it is: You've noticed a mistake a few stitches back in the same row you're still on—and you want to fix it before you go any further.

How to fix it: It's almost like knitting in reverse—you want to move stitches from your right needle back onto your left.

1. Push the tip of your left needle into the bump below the first stitch on the right needle. Move the stitch off the right needle.

2. Then pull the strand of yarn to take out the stitch. Repeat for each stitch you want to take out.

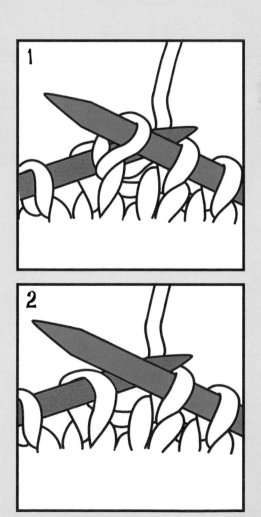

21

Adding More Yarn

What it is: You've used up a whole ball of yarn—but your project isn't finished yet!

How to do it: Always add more yarn at the start of a new row. Put the right needle through the first stitch on the left needle. Then loop the new yarn around the right needle (instead of using the yarn you're running out of). Knit the stitch like normal, then pull all the ends tight. Keep knitting, making sure to use the long end of the new yarn and not the old yarn. When the project is done, sew in the ends along the side.

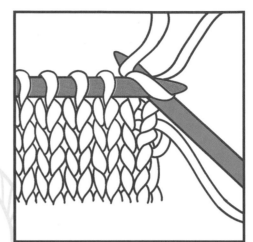

Taking Out Rows & Putting Stitches Back on the Needle

What it is: When you've got a lot of stitches to take out—a few rows or more—ripping out whole rows is a much quicker (and easier!) way to do it than taking out each stitch individually.

How to do it: The key to ripping out rows without dropping stitches is to be careful! First, take all the stitches off your needle. Then gently pull the long tail of yarn. Watch carefully as it slips out of each stitch. Keep pulling the yarn (remember—go slow!) until you've taken out all the rows you want. Then slip the needle back into each stitch. When you knit the next row, make sure all the stitches are back on the needle in the right direction. If they feel tighter than usual, chances are they're twisted. To fix a twisted stitch, simply slip it off the needle, twist it around, and put it back on the needle. That's it!

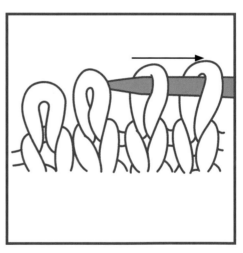

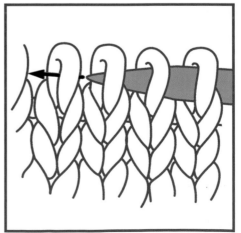

Gauge

What it is: Gauge is simple to understand—and super-important to your knitting projects. Basically, gauge tells you how many stitches fit into a certain measurement. Everyone's gauge is slightly different—some people knit more tightly; some people knit more loosely. Your gauge will change depending on the size of your needles and the kind of yarn you use. That's why it's so important to figure out your gauge before starting a pattern. Here's the gauge used in this book:

Garter: 18 stitches and 36 rows = 4"
Stockinette: 18 stitches and 24 rows = 4"
Rib: 25 stitches and 24 rows = 4"

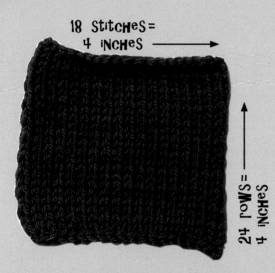

18 STITCHES = 4 INCHES ⟶

24 ROWS = 4 INCHES

How to measure it: Knit a sample piece with the same dimensions as the gauge listed (in the example above, you'd cast on 18 stitches and knit for 36 rows). That should give you a 4 x 4 inch square (or a close approximation!). If your sample is much bigger than that, you are a loose knitter. You can adjust by using smaller knitting needles. If your sample is much smaller than that, you are a tight knitter. Trying using needles that are a size larger.

Measuring

What it is: The best way to find out if your knitting is on track!

How to do it: Lay the knitted piece on a flat surface, and gently smooth it with your hands. You can use your hands to shape the knitting by pulling gently on it if you need to. Then measure the length or width with a tape measure.

Buying More Yarn and Reading Labels

When you're all out of yarn, head down to the yarn store to buy more! Bring the pattern so that you can find exactly the right kind of yarn for it. Yarn labels usually have a really helpful diagram on them. You can use the diagram to make sure you're buying the right size yarn—and enough yarn to finish your project, too!

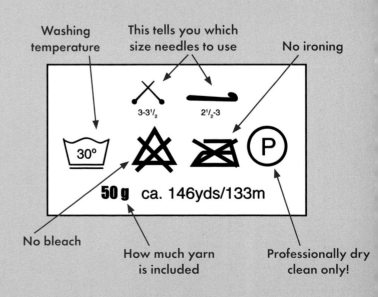

Washing temperature

This tells you which size needles to use

No ironing

3-3½   2½-3

30°

50 g   ca. 146yds/133m

P

No bleach

How much yarn is included

Professionally dry clean only!

Stitch Styles

CHECK OUT SOME GREAT STITCHES YOU CAN MAKE FROM COMBINING KNIT AND PURL!

Garter

Garter stitch produces bumpy texture in distinct rows, and both sides look the same. With a little practice, you'll be able to knit garter stitch on autopilot!

How to do it:

Easy—just knit every row.

Stockinette

Stockinette produces a smooth, flat front and a bumpy back—unlike garter stitch, you'll definitely be able to tell which side is which. Stockinette also makes the edges curl. You can use this to your advantage on some patterns (for the brim of the Cozy Hat or the cord strap for the Pretty Purse). If you don't want the edges to curl, though, have an adult help you iron them flat with an iron on a very low setting.

How to do it:

Row 1: Knit.

Row 2: Purl.

Repeat rows 1 and 2 until you're done—that's it!

Moss

Moss stitch is also called seed stitch. Alternating knit and purl makes it really strong—which is why it's a good choice for the Sturdy Strap in the Pretty Purse pattern.

How to do it:

Row 1: Start off with a knit stitch or purl stitch, and alternate for the entire row.

Row 2 (odd number of stitches): Repeat Row 1.

Row 2 (even number of stitches): Do the opposite of Row 1. If you started with a knit stitch, start Row 2 with a purl; if you started with a purl stitch, begin with a knit stitch.

Rib

Rib stitch is *very* stretchy. It's perfect for the iPod Case, because it will stretch to fit your iPod!

How to do it:

1 x 1 Rib

Row 1: Knit one stitch, purl one stitch, and repeat for the entire row.

The pattern for the second row depends on how many cast-on stitches you have.

Row 2 (even number of stitches): Repeat Row 1.

Row 2 (odd number of stitches): Purl one stitch, knit one stitch, and repeat for the entire row—it's the opposite of Row 1.

2 x 2 Rib

Follow the same basic pattern as 1 x 1 rib, just make sure to knit two stitches and purl two stitches (instead of just one) at each step.

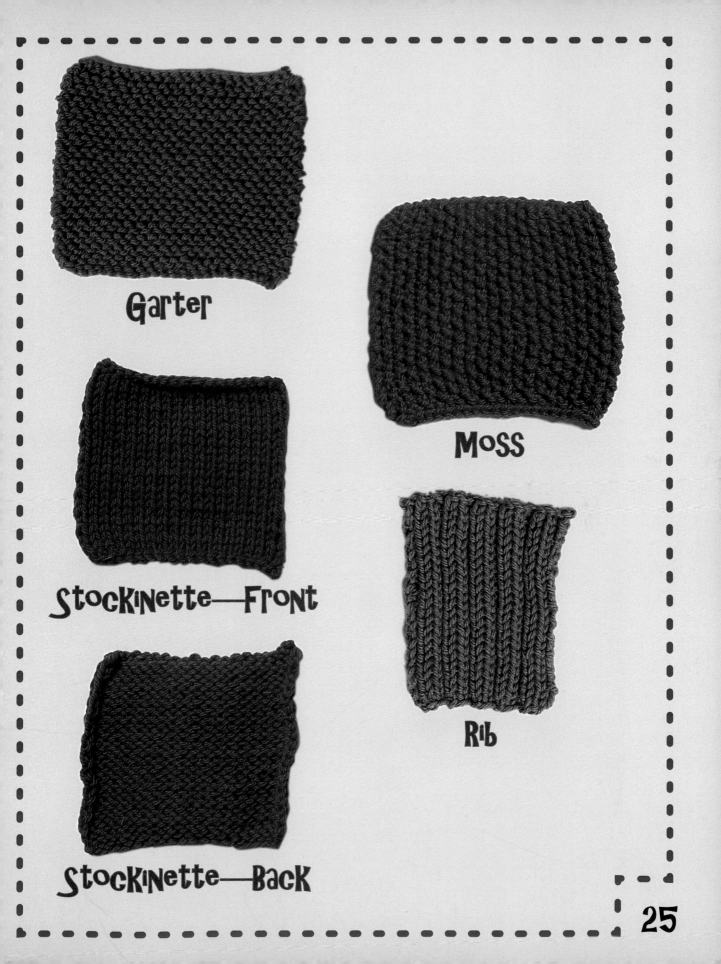

Garter

Moss

Stockinette—Front

Rib

Stockinette—Back

SaSSy ScarF

THIS SCARF IS SUPER-EASY TO MAKE—JUST KEEP KNITTING UNTIL YOU DECIDE IT'S LONG ENOUGH. THEN CAST OFF!

26

Dimensions: 4.5 x 48–60 inches
Stitch: Garter (knit every row)
Materials: About 127-225 yards of yarn (depending on how long you want your scarf); size 8 knitting needles; yarn needle

SCARF

1. Cast on 20 stitches. (For a long and skinny scarf, cast on 12 stitches.) If you want stripes, read those directions now.

2. Knit every stitch in the first row.

3. Knit every stitch in the second row.

4. Keep knitting every row until the scarf is as long as you want it to be (48-60 inches is a good length).

5. Cast off.

6. Sew in all ends.

STRIPES

Stripes are easy to add to anything you knit! It's just like adding a new ball of yarn. You can knit thin stripes or thick stripes, evenly spaced stripes or stripes that are all over the place—it's up to you!

1. For the first stripe, knit until the section is as thick as you want your stripe to be.

2. Join a new color of yarn and knit until the second stripe is the thickness you want.

3. Repeat, with as many colors as you want, until the scarf is finished. Make sure to always join the new yarn on the same side of the scarf!

4. Sew in all ends.

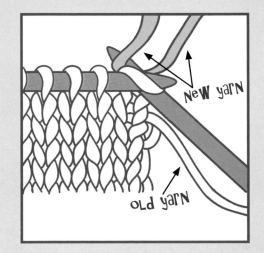

NEW yarn

OLD yarn

FRINGE

When the scarf is finished, you can add fringe if you want. The easiest way to add fringe is with a crochet hook.

1. Decide how long you want your fringe to be. Four inches is a good fringe length for a scarf.

2. Cut lengths of yarn that are twice as long as you want the fringe. For example, cut each piece of yarn 8 inches long if you want 4-inch fringe.

3. For each bunch of fringe, fold a few pieces of yarn (five or six) in half. If you want thicker fringe, use more yarn.

4. Use the crochet hook to pull the folded yarn through the bottom corner of the scarf. Don't pull the yarn all the way through—just enough so that the loop of yarn is on one side of the scarf and the tails are on the other.

5. Slip the ends of the yarn through the loop, and pull tight.

6. Repeat steps 3–5 for each bunch of fringe, making sure to space them evenly across the edge of the scarf. When you've finished one end of the scarf, go back and add fringe to the other.

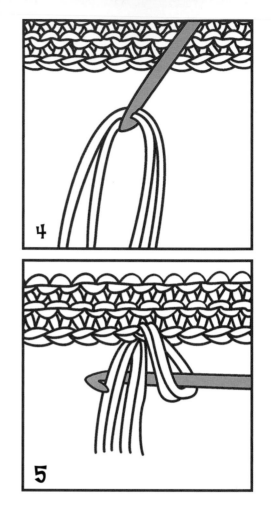

This was the first time Bonnie put fringe on a scarf. It looks so great that she added fringe to all her other scarves, too!

Scarf Styles

Scarves are a perfect project to experiment with different knitting stitches—their long, even shape lets you try out a new stitch without having to worry about adapting a complicated pattern. Experimenting with several different stitches will help you pick the best one for your yarn.

These scarves look totally different, but they are all garter stitch! It all depends on the kind of yarn and the needle size you use. For a lacy scarf, like the green one, use thin yarn on big needles. The rainbow scarf looks fluffy because the yarn is made up of little loops—check it out:

Rib stitch makes this scarf extra stretchy and cozy.

Megan used moss stitch to show all the awesome colors and textures of the yarn.

Pretty Purses

Time to design! Make this purse all your own. It can be big or small. The flap that closes it can be pointed or straight. Even the strap can be customized—it's all up to you!

Dimensions: 6 x 4 inches (small purse);
6 x 8 inches (big purse)
Stitch: Garter (knit every row)
Materials: About 60 yards of yarn for the small purse or 120 yards of yarn for the big purse; size 8 knitting needles; yarn needle; safety pin; button; sewing needle and thread

PURSE

1. Cast on 27 stitches.
2. Knit every row for 8 inches for the small purse; 16 inches for the big purse.
3. Decide which kind of flap you want to make (pointed or straight), and follow the directions for it.

POINTED FLAP

Row 1: Knit
Row 2: Knit 2 together, knit to last 2 stitches, knit 2 together (25 stitches left)
Row 3: Knit
Row 4: Knit 2 together, knit to last 2 stitches, knit 2 together (23 stitches left)
Row 5: Knit
Row 6: Knit 2 together, knit to last 2 stitches, knit 2 together (21 stitches left)
Row 7: Knit
Row 8: Knit 2 together, knit to last 2 stitches, knit 2 together (19 stitches left)
Row 9: Knit
Row 10: Knit 2 together, knit to last 2 stitches, knit 2 together (17 stitches left)
Row 11: Knit
Row 12: Knit 2 together, knit to last 2 stitches, knit 2 together (15 stitches left)
Row 13: Knit
Row 14: Knit 2 together, knit to last 2 stitches, knit 2 together (13 stitches left)
Row 15: Knit

Row 16: Knit 2 together, knit to last 2 stitches, knit 2 together (11 stitches left)
Row 17: Knit
Row 18: Knit 2 together, knit to last 2 stitches, knit 2 together (9 stitches left)
Row 19: Knit
Row 20: *Buttonhole Row:* Knit 2 together, knit 2 stitches, yarn over, knit 2 together, knit 1, knit 2 together (7 stitches left)
Row 21: Knit
Row 22: Knit 2 together, knit to last 2 stitches, knit 2 together (5 stitches left)
Row 23: Knit
Row 24: Knit 2 together, knit 1, knit 2 together (3 stitches left)
Row 25: Knit
Row 26: Cast off

Knit Tip: Yarn-Overs

Yarn-overs make little holes in your knitting. You can use them to make buttonholes or as eyelet to weave ribbon through. They're exactly what they sound like: Between two stitches, wrap the yarn over (around) the right needle, then continue knitting like normal.

Bonnie thought her strap was too long, so she tied a knot in it and now she's good to go.

A Sturdy Strap

A curly cord

Get the Point!

Play It Straight!

STRAIGHT-EDGED FLAP

Knit for 16 rows.

Row 17: *Buttonhole Row:* Knit 13 stitches, yarn over, knit 2 together, knit to end of row.

Row 18: Knit.

Row 19: Knit.

Row 20: Cast off.

CURLY CORD

1. Cast on 3 stitches.

2. Work in stockinette stitch (see page 24) for about 30 inches, or however long you want the strap to be.

3. Cast off. (The edges of the strap will curl to make it look like a cord.)

STURDY STRAP

1. Cast on 5 stitches.

2. Work in moss stitch (see page 24) for about 30 inches, or however long you want the strap to be.

3. Cast off.

FINISHING

1. Sew in all ends on the purse.

2. Fold the purse in half so that the front and back of the purse are the same length (4 inches for the small purse, 8 inches for the big purse). Don't include the flap in this measurement; it will extend off the back of the purse.

3. Sew up each side of the purse.

4. Fold over the flap, and put a safety pin in the purse where the buttonhole in the flap hits the purse.

5. Sew a button onto the purse where the safety pin is.

6. Sew the strap onto each side of the purse (you can use the tails attached to each end of the strap to sew it on).

Megan *loves* purple and pink, so of course she wanted a purple and pink bag! Check out the matching mini-purse she made on page 34.

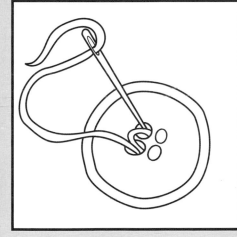

Knit Tip: Knit 2 Together

Knitting two stitches together is technically called a decrease—it will give you one less stitch than you had before. This is especially useful when you are making yarn-overs, since the yarn-over will give you one more stitch than you had before. To knit two stitches together, put the right needle into the first two stitches on the left needle. Then knit like normal, making sure to push both stitches off the left needle instead of just the first one.

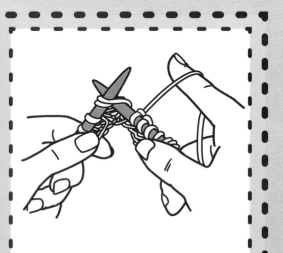

MINI-PURSES

THIS CUTE PURSE KEEPS TINY THINGS SAFE—FROM LOOSE CHANGE TO A LITTLE LIPSTICK TO YOUR SCHOOL I.D. YOU CAN COORDINATE IT TO MATCH THE BIG PURSE. IF YOU WANT, KNIT A SUPER-SKINNY CORD OUT OF TWO STITCHES FOR A FEW INCHES, AND ATTACH THE MINI-PURSE TO THE BIG PURSE. THEN IT REALLY WON'T GET LOST! (CHECK OUT PAGES 31 AND 33 FOR INFO ON HOW TO KNIT TWO STITCHES TOGETHER OR DO A YARN-OVER.)

Dimensions: 2.5 x 2.5 inches
Stitch: Garter (knit every row)
Materials: About 23 yards of yarn; size 8 needles; yarn needle; button; sewing needle and thread

PURSE

1. Cast on 13 stitches.

2. Knit for 5 inches.

3. Decide which kind of flap you want to make— straight or pointed—and follow those directions.

POINTED FLAP

Row 1: Knit

Row 2: Knit 2 together, knit to last 2 stitches, knit 2 together (11 stitches left)

Row 3: Knit

Row 4: Knit 2 together, knit to last 2 stitches, knit 2 together (9 stitches left)

Row 5: Knit

Row 6: Knit 2 together, knit to last 2 stitches, knit 2 together (7 stitches left)

Row 7: Knit

Row 8: *Buttonhole Row:* Knit 2 together, knit 1, yarn over, knit 2 together, knit 2 together (5 stitches left)

Row 9: Knit

Row 10: Knit 2 together, knit 1, knit 2 together (3 stitches left)

Row 11: Knit

Row 12: Cast off

STRAIGHT FLAP

Knit for 5 rows

Row 6: *Buttonhole Row:* Knit 6 stitches, yarn over, knit 2 together, knit to end of row

Row 7: Knit

Row 8: Knit

Row 9: Cast off

FINISHING

1. Fold the mini-purse in half so that the front and the back are the same length, 2.5 inches each. Don't include the flap in this measurement; it will extend off the back of the mini-purse.

2. Fold over the flap and place a safety pin in the purse where the buttonhole on the flap hits the purse.

3. Sew a button where the safety pin is placed.

Straight flap

To make thin stripes like these, knit two rows in each color.

Pointed flap

iPod Case

Carry your tunes in style with this awesome iPod case! Soft yarn keeps the window safe from scratches, while two fun flaps hold your iPod snug inside. (Check out pages 31 and 33 for info on how to knit two stitches together or do a yarn-over.)

• •

Dimensions: 3.25 x 4 inches
Stitch: Rib (knit one, purl one)
Materials: About 32 yards of yarn; size 8 needles; two large safety pins; yarn needle; two small buttons; sewing needle and thread

FRONT

1. Cast on 20 stitches.
2. Knit the first stitch, then purl the second stitch. Repeat across the whole row (knit, purl, knit, purl, and so on).
3. Repeat this pattern for every row until the case measures 4.25 inches.
4. Cast off.

BACK

1. Follow the directions for the front up to Step 3.

Make the right strap

2. Work the first six stitches according to the pattern: knit, purl, knit, purl, knit, purl.
3. Then cast off 8 stitches.

Make the left strap

4. Work the last six stitches according to the pattern: knit, purl, knit, purl, knit, purl.
5. Place the six stitches on the right side of the case onto a safety pin—you'll knit this strap later.

Work the left strap

6. Work 6 rows in 1 x 1 rib according to the pattern.
7. On the 7th row: Knit 1, purl 1, knit 1, yarn over, knit 2 together, knit 1. This makes a buttonhole.
8. On the 8th row: Work 1 row in 1 x 1 rib.
9. Cast off.

Work the right strap

10. Put the stitches for the right strap back on the needle, add new yarn, and work 6 rows in 1 x 1 rib.
11. On the 7th row: Knit 1, purl 1, knit 1, yarn over, knit 2 together, knit 1. This makes a buttonhole.
12. On the 8th row: Work 1 row in 1 x 1 rib.
13. Cast off.

FINISHING

1. Sew in all ends.
2. Sew the front and the back of the case together—the left side, the bottom, and the right side. Don't sew the top edges together.
3. Fold each strap over and put a safety pin in the front of the case where the buttonhole lands.
4. Sew a button where each safety pin is placed.

KNit Tip: KNit or PurL?

When you're mixing knit and purl stitches, how can you tell if you should knit or purl the next stitch? You can usually figure it out by looking at the stitch you're working on. A purl stitch looks like this—

and you'll want to purl it for rib, knit it for moss. A knit stitch looks like this—

and you'll want to knit it for rib, purl it for moss.

iPod Mini Case

I F YOU WANT AN iPOD MINI CASE, FOLLOW THESE DIRECTIONS
INSTEAD. THE DIFFERENCES IN THE PATTERN ARE PRETTY MINI—
BUT THEY REALLY MATTER!

Dimensions: 2 x 3.5 inches
Stitch: Rib (knit one, purl one)
Materials: About 22 yards of yarn; size 8
needles; yarn needle; one small button; sewing
needle and thread

FRONT

1. Cast on 14 stitches.

2. Knit the first stitch, then purl the second stitch.
Repeat across the whole row (knit, purl, knit, purl,
and so on).

3. Repeat this pattern until the front measures 3.75
inches.

4. Cast off.

BACK

1. Follow the directions for the front up to Step 3.

Make the strap

2. Cast off 6 stitches.

3. Work the remaining 8 stitches in 1 x 1 rib for
1.5 inches.

4. *Buttonhole Row:* Work 4 stitches according to
pattern, yarn over, knit 2 together, then work the
last 2 stitches according to the pattern.

5. Work 1 row in 1 x 1 rib.

6. Cast off.

FINISHING

1. Sew in all ends.

2. Sew the front and the back of the case
together—the left side, the bottom, and the right
side. Don't sew the top edges together. Make
sure the strap folds over the left side of the case,
so that the earplug jack isn't covered.

3. Fold the strap over and put a safety pin in the
front of the case where the buttonhole lands.

4. Sew a button where the safety pin is placed.

CELL PHONE POUCH

THERE ARE TWO WAYS TO MAKE THIS CUTE CELL PHONE POUCH. BOTH ARE WORKED IN STOCKINETTE STITCH, BUT ONE USES YARN-OVERS TO CREATE *EYELETS* (LITTLE HOLES); YOU CAN WEAVE PRETTY RIBBON THROUGH THE EYELET TO ADD A NICE FINISHING TOUCH. THE OTHER PATTERN IS STRAIGHT STOCKINETTE THROUGHOUT. (CHECK OUT PAGES 31 AND 33 FOR INFO ON HOW TO KNIT TWO STITCHES TOGETHER OR DO A YARN-OVER.)

Dimensions: 3 x 4.25 inches (case); 4 inches (strap)

Stitch: Stockinette (knit one row, purl one row)

Materials: About 24 yards of yarn; size 8 knitting needles; yarn needle; button; sewing needle and thread; 12 inches ribbon (optional)

CASE

1. Cast on 14 stitches.

2. Row 1: Knit.

3. Row 2: Purl.

4. Row 3:

For ribbon trim: Knit 2, yarn over, knit 2 together, knit 1. Yarn over, knit 2 together, knit 1. Yarn over, knit 2 together, knit 1. Yarn over, knit 2 together, knit 1.

No ribbon trim: Knit.

5. Work in stockinette stitch (knit one row, purl one row, repeat) until the pouch measures 8 inches, ending with a purl row.

6. For ribbon trim: Knit 2, yarn over, knit 2 together, knit 1. Yarn over, knit 2 together, knit 1. Yarn over, knit 2 together, knit 1. Yarn over, knit 2 together, knit 1.

No ribbon trim: Knit.

7. Purl one row.

8. Knit one row.

9. Cast off.

STRAP

Ribbon trim:

Cast on 3 stitches

Row 1: Knit

Row 2: Purl

Row 3: Knit 1, yarn over, knit 2 together

Row 4: Purl

Row 5: Knit

Row 6: Purl

Row 7: Knit 1, yarn over, knit 2 together

Row 8: Purl

Row 9: Knit

Row 10: Purl

Row 11: Knit 1, yarn over, knit 2 together

Row 12: Purl

Row 13: Knit

Row 14: Purl

Row 15: *Buttonhole Row:* Knit 1, yarn over, knit 2 together

Row 16: Knit

Row 17: Knit

Row 18: Knit

Cast off

Ribbon trim and a sweet little button look great . . .

but you don't have to get all frilly!

STRAP (CONTINUED)

No ribbon trim:

Cast on 3 stitches.

Work in stockinette for 14 rows.

Row 15: *Buttonhole Row:* Knit 1, yarn over, knit 2 together.

Row 16: Knit.

Row 17: Knit.

Row 18: Knit.

Cast off.

FINISHING

With ribbon trim

1. Sew in all ends.

2. Sew the two sides together, making sure the yarn-overs on both sides match up.

3. Weave the ribbon through the yarn-overs and tie it into a small bow in the front.

4. Weave the ribbon through the first three yarn-overs in the strap and sew it in place with a needle and thread.

5. Sew the strap to the left side of the case.

6. Sew a button onto the right side of the case using a sewing needle and thread.

Without ribbon trim

1. Sew in all ends.

2. Sew the two sides together.

3. Sew the strap to the left side of the case.

4. Using a sewing needle and thread, sew a button onto the right side of the case.

Cozy Hat

The bottom edge of this cool hat curls up to make a cute brim! Knitting two stitches together makes a star pattern on the crown of the hat (find out how on page 33). For extra fun, top off your hat with a matching pom-pom!

Dimensions: 8.5 inches long, 22 inches around
Stitch: Stockinette (knit one row, purl one row)
Materials: About 115 yards of yarn; size 8 needles; yarn needle

1. Cast on 88 stitches. Carefully count to make sure you have 88 stitches—you might want to count them twice just to be sure. Your needle will be very full, so count your stitches every few rows to make sure you haven't lost any.

2. Knit the first row. Purl the second row. Repeat until the hat is 7.5 inches long when it is unrolled.

3. Now start decreasing to round off the top of the hat:

Row 1: Knit 6 stitches, knit 2 together. Repeat for the rest of the row. You will have 77 stitches left.

Row 2: Purl.

Row 3: Knit 5 stitches, knit 2 together. Repeat for the rest of the row. You will have 66 stitches left.

Row 4: Purl.

Row 5: Knit 4 stitches, knit 2 together. Repeat for the rest of the row. You will have 55 stitches left.

Row 6: Purl.

Row 7: Knit 3 stitches, knit 2 together. Repeat for the rest of the row. You will have 44 stitches left.

Row 8: Purl.

Row 9: Knit 2 stitches, knit 2 together. Repeat for the rest of the row. You will have 33 stitches left.

Row 10: Purl.

Row 11: Knit 1 stitch, knit 2 together. Repeat for the rest of the row. You will have 22 stitches left.

Row 12: Purl.

Row 13: Knit 2 stitches together. Repeat for the rest of the row. You will have 11 stitches left.

Row 14: Purl.

FINISHING

1. Cut the tail of the yarn so that it is about 18 inches long. Using a yarn needle, thread the yarn through the remaining 11 stitches on the needle and pull tight to close them up.

2. Starting at the top, use the tail of the yarn to sew the two sides of the hat together. Sew in any other ends.

POM-POMS

POM-POMS ARE A FUN (AND EASY!) WAY TO TOP OFF A HAT—ESPECIALLY IF YOU HAVE YARN LEFT OVER. MAKE THE POM-POM AS BIG OR LITTLE AS YOU WANT.

1. Start by winding the yarn around your fingers (just like you're winding the yarn into a ball).

2. Keep wrapping! The more yarn you wrap around your fingers, the puffier your pom-pom will be.

3. Carefully slip the yarn off your fingers. Tightly tie a 6-inch piece of yarn around the center of the yarn. (It's a good idea to make a double knot.)

4. Cut the yarn loops on either side of the knot. You might need to give your pom-pom a trim all around to make it really puff out. Ta-da—a puffy pom-pom!

GLITZ UP YOUR KNITS!

DON'T BE AFRAID TO MIX THINGS UP AND MAKE YOUR KNITS YOUR OWN. IF YOU LIKE SPARKLES, SEW SOME SEQUINS OR BEADS ONTO YOUR PROJECTS. YOU CAN ADD RIBBON TO ALMOST ANY PROJECT—JUST ADD A FEW YARN-OVERS ALONG THE EDGE AND YOU CAN WEAVE VELVET, SILK, OR SATIN RIBBON THROUGH IT (SEE PAGES 31 AND 41 FOR MORE INFO).

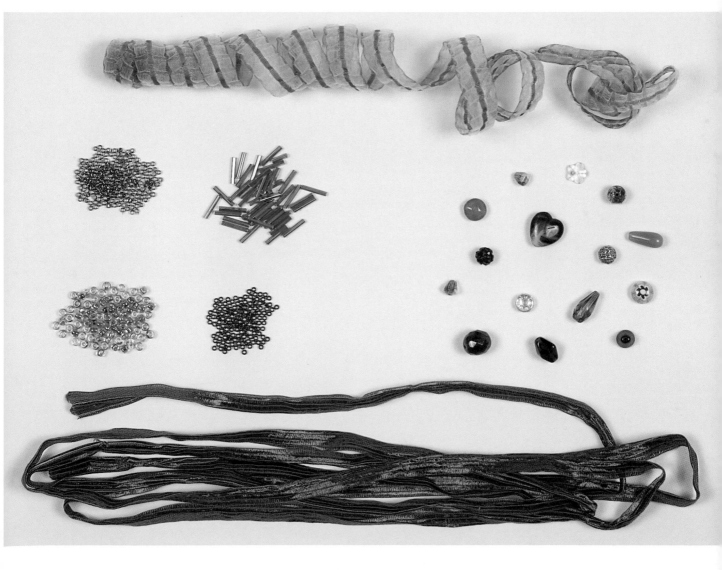

FLOWERS

HERE'S A FAB FLOWER THAT YOU CAN KNIT UP REALLY FAST! PLAY AROUND WITH DIFFERENT COLORS FOR THE PETALS UNTIL YOU FIND YOUR FAVORITES. (SEE PAGE 33 FOR INFORMATION ON KNITTING TWO STITCHES TOGETHER.)

This flower has eight petals—four on top and four on bottom!

For each petal:

1. Cast on 4 stitches.

2. Knit one row.

3. Knit one row, increasing one stitch at each end. (6 stitches)

4. Knit one row.

5. Knit one row, increasing one stitch at each end. (8 stitches)

6. Knit one row.

7. Knit 2 together, knit 4 stitches, knit 2 together. (6 stitches)

8. Knit 2 together, knit 2 stitches, knit 2 together. (4 stitches)

9. Knit 2 together, knit 2 together. (2 stitches)

10. Knit one row.

11. Cast off.

Repeat steps 1–11 for each flower petal. You'll want five petals at least, but you can make lots of petals for a full, fluffy flower! Sew the petals together at the pointy end. If you want, make a tiny yellow pom-pom for the flower's center (see page 44) or sew bright yellow yarn over the center of the flower.

Increasing

When you increase, you are adding an extra stitch to a project you're already working on. Here's an easy way to increase at the edge of your knitting.

1. Start the same way as knitting: Put your right needle through the first loop on the left needle and wrap the yarn around the right needle.

2. Pull the right needle out of the left needle, but don't push the stitch off the left needle. Instead, put the right needle through the back of the left needle.

3. Wrap the yarn around the right needle again.

4. Move the right needle back through the stitch.

5. Now you can slip the stitch off the left needle. You'll have two stitches on the right needle instead of just one!

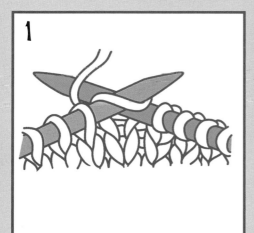

1

2

KNit beHiNd the Stitch

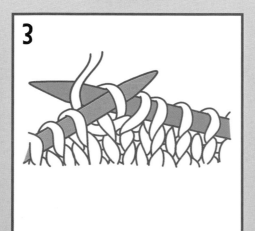

3

INdeX